beyond the paneling

poems by

Christine A. Brooks

Finishing Line Press
Georgetown, Kentucky

beyond the paneling

For Mom

Copyright © 2021 by Christine A. Brooks
ISBN 978-1-64662-475-1 First Edition
All rights reserved under International and Pan-American Copyright Conventions.
No part of this book may be reproduced in any manner whatsoever without written
permission from the publisher, except in the case of brief quotations embodied in
critical articles and reviews.

ACKNOWLEDGMENTS

Door Is A Jar, *Death & Doughnuts*, Summer 2019
The Cabinet of Heed, *White Light* Issue 19, 2019
Door Is A Jar, *Vespers*, January 2019
The Cabinet of Heed, *The Price* September 2019
Door Is A Jar, *Life, I Don't Believe* Fall 2019
Poethead, *house of beauty, nothingness, Newbury Street, A Date with the Lord, Fireflies*, 2019
Multiplicity Magazine, *the inside & out*, April 2020
Neologism Poetry, *morning wood*, February 2020
Pub House Books, *communion*, January 2020

Publisher: Leah Huete de Maines
Editor: Christen Kincaid
Cover Art: Christine A. Brooks
Author Photo: Christine A. Brooks
Cover Design: Elizabeth Maines McCleavy

Printed in the USA on acid-free paper.
Order online: www.finishinglinepress.com
also available on amazon.com

Author inquiries and mail orders:
Finishing Line Press
P. O. Box 1626
Georgetown, Kentucky 40324
U. S. A.

Table of Contents

The Inside & Out 1

the price 3

Fireflies 5

Breath 6

Life's Circle 7

A Date with the Lord 8

Death & Doughnuts 11

Vespers 13

White Light 14

Newbury Street 17

Noise 18

Neighbors 19

beyond the paneling 20

Opposites 21

ravenous 23

I don't believe 24

life 25

nothingness 27

house of beauty 28

faces 30

Desi 31

communion 33

on being small 35

morning wood 36

The Inside & Out

Inside a drop of
  rain,
 in this place of
drowned granite & smooth
cobble

looking out,

from melancholy tears
blown in
from the
Irish Sea
golden Kings walk among
us
as freely as those pale
shadows
that have most unwillingly
gone
ahead if only, to walk us
home

not a mindful breath
away,
like the coos from unseen
birds
in the mossy roots of the
grand twisted trees on the
green

but, instead they
  amble
freely, breaking bread,
proud,

knowing
—finally

we have found a
place,
where prisms of
drink and
foreign silence
let them be seen &
heard
inside & out

the price

The moths
　cursed at, by you
that gathered 'round your
old
porch light
that I switched on so
you, would not

stumble or tumble or
look otherwise,

foolish

my already tattered hoodie,
now covered in
mud,
from the puddle I laid it
across so your new
sneakers, could
stay
new and

—white.

and my body,
that I
threw in front of a train,
hoping it would slow down
so, you would be
on time
for
　afternoon mass

all reminded me, that
as you dipped your
French fries in my blood &
raised your Red Stripe to
my many shortcomings

I was
 free

to join the dancing
moths in my soiled
hoodie and gather up my
blood by the
—light

of the moon.

Fireflies

I recall them,
as beacons of hope & faith
 from my childhood

buzzing and banging,
gently
 against the glass walls of my
Nana's mason jar
lighting the way, selflessly
 just for a moment, a heartbeat
 tick between the tock
contained.

I unscrew the lid,
 set them free, and
watch
them blink into the hush
of the late summer's night.

I recall them,
these memories

 not as the embers
they were—hovering, clanking
 against the mental box I
put them in,
as they feverishly tried to burn
 down
 my construction paper
childhood.

I recall them, as
 —fireflies

Breath

A breeze, gentle
　—just learning, new and
warm
how to be the
howling wind, cold and
　unforgiving
will not stop to pick up
　the papers it tosses
about
but
it will always be careful
not to damage the
　　pages

Life's Circle

Cocktail napkin
  f l a t
Held down not by
the glass, but by the soggy
ring of where the glass once
  was

A Date with the Lord

the morning I met the
Lord was exactly as I
imagined
it would
be.

the air,
   both, briny & candied
plump with salt from the
Irish Sea &
sweet from the
River Liffey
tickled as I inhaled
but that did not stop me from
breathing in
   life.

some, even most,
—maybe,
would not find it
pleasant or pleasing, but
for me it was
perfection,
on an early summer Dublin morning,
before businesses opened, but not before business
happened,

   with horse drawn carriages & guitar players
& those offering blessings of good fortune,
wishing me well,
after several donations.

I paid the price,
   I owed
maybe even, a little more than that
which pleased us both
   —equally.

God bless you said more than money could buy
   maybe
I'm hungry, she said, although
she looked neither the kind
 of person to offer a blessing that had the chance of
sticking, or someone whose dinner plate was
empty often

but I had seen her before,
believed her then, that blessing
so, I dropped another heavy coin into her
   cup, clanging
& shuffled along Dawson Street
because,
      it mattered not

I had a date with the Lord after-all & had no time to
 wonder
if the woman I never thought I would see again
—but did
could grant the wish offered up to
Eire.

finally, I had come upon the Mansion House
more than what
it seemed, initially
set back without the warmth
& cool of thick mossy blades
of emerald patchwork

still though, warm enough
welcoming enough, although no
mat said so, and the giant
brass, doorbell that rang to the
unknown, still, did
not dissuade me from my
date with the Lord.

I had an appointment
   after all.

my clothes, comfortable but
not my finest, reminded
me, without knowledge or
preconceived notions that
   I was,
home
in a place that accepted me
as is.

and in that moment,
those moments,
as we sipped tea
& the outside came to life
I was
   —happy.

Death and Doughnuts

Hello there

you look like my daughter, she has your eyes.
Do you know her?

Forgive me lady,
I have forgotten your name.
Have I already asked you?

You look like my daughter, she has your eyes
have I mentioned that?
You look so sad
are you alright?

I had a doughnut today
Did you know that?
I don't know who brought them, but
she looked like my daughter, she had the
same
eyes.

I wish I could go home,
I don't like it here.
Where am I?

I wish I could have a doughnut
Glazed ones are my favorite
Do you like doughnuts lady?
Forgive me, I have forgotten your name.

Maybe you could tell my daughter something
for me?
You look kind, I can see it in your eyes.
Could you tell her I love her and that I would love
    another doughnut.

Glazed are my favorite.

Forgive me,
did you mention your name?
I do hope my daughter comes soon.
She looks like you, she is bringing me
doughnuts.

Oh, look the doughnuts are right here,
by my bed.
Did my daughter stop by?
Was I sleeping?

Forgive me.

Vespers

On the rare warm, quiet night
That comes along when spring is ready to push us forward, but
Summer is not quite ready to catch us—he prays.
On these nights, windows open
under the covers I can hear him.

In the time just before the dark of night shrouds dusk completely,
the robins and the
sparrows chirp their night time lullabies.
They sing their soulful songs knowing that soon he will be there,
watching, guiding, and
standing guard over their homes of sticks and scraps.

Dishes clank just outside my window as some neighbors are just finishing dinner, and
lights dim to the other side as the tired tuck in early and hope for a restful night listening
to the crickets as they begin their own symphony of chirps.

Over the hum of the box fan and the wind in the giant American Yellowwood tree
outside my window, he prays.

From his moon porch, the man prays every night,
for another night
that the birds will sing and the crickets will chirp, and the tired get rest
Tonight, like all nights, the man in the moon can only watch, and pray
and hope that
we all awake to
peace.

White Light

When I was younger
seven or eight, maybe
even
younger than
that,
the thunder came rolling
in

over our house that
had been
dropped
on the outskirts of
 urban-ia
landing on a street mostly
forgotten.

 28 Ionia rattled and
 shivered, but
never, not ever
crumbled from the
booms,
or from the
bolts.

I hid from the loud claps
 house shaking, knees
knockin',
under the bed, hoping
for time to grow longer and
longer
as I counted the
seconds
between the
growls and
bright flashes of
 white.

Come out, you say
the angels are just bowling, no
need to quiver,
  no need to shake.

Look at the dark sky
streaked
with white, even in pitch
there is
    —light.

Sometimes, it isn't thunder
that rumbles and grumbles, or
lightening
that flashes and

 flickers our lights

No, not at all.

The angels are
bowling
I remind myself

and when I do
I am with you again
  in your arms
starched white nurse's cap
  Bobby-pinned high atop
 your salt and pepper
Bouffant hairdo

Even in pitch there is
light.

Even in pitch there is
light.

Even in pitch
there is
  light.

Newbury Street

my Papa smoked a pipe &
 watched hockey with the sound
off, in another
room
from where I played   quietly
with my Lincoln Logs

Nana, who was supposed to die
long before I came around,
had the doctors been right about
her throat cancer

knitted & clucked trying to keep her
mouth moist somehow since her body
stopped making saliva

she made gowumpki's
he gave butterfly kisses &

we lived with them one
summer, so very long
ago

most days I had a bellyache

nervous, she's just nervous
my mother would say

   dismissing my pain, probably
to dismiss her own

it didn't matter though &
eventually we moved, but my
bellyache stayed

Noise

it's impossible to read a
chapter, a poem or even
think straight with all the
god damned noise & the
the fucking dogs barking

    yipping at each other
incessantly

until finally, the neighbors
are yelling at them to be quiet, more dogs bark at
the yelling neighbors,

more yipping

even more yipping
and yelling

until finally, I have no choice
accept to shut the god
damned window in this god
damned house and
wonder

what the fuck got those dogs
barking in the first place

Neighbors

not much happened on Ionia Street,
not much worth
mentioning   anyway

our only guest was tragedy
and even that didn't visit
often

one girl with long blonde hair was
hit by a car crossing the street,
her brother not long after
flipped his Jeep

they both died before they
were old enough to drink

or get married
or have children
or buy a house
or have a job they cursed

or lose those things

not much happened though

mostly we just never
knew what was going on
    —behind closed doors

beyond the paneling—

beyond the paneling,
past the glow of the yellow
light, cast from a bronze
colored glass shade

    and far from the
dank stankiness of my hair

    pillowcases & sheets

a life for me exists

but for now, right now
in this very moment

I can't help but wonder
    how the fuck

I got here

Opposites

my mother would have boiled
over in rage & sadness
 if she knew
I looked into my
biological beginnings

if she knows now, if the
dead can know anything at all

I think she would like it,
knowing Emily Dickinson was
a

    distant cousin

she would find it delicate &
classy & nod her head in
agreement that NOW she
understood

but she didn't

she couldn't

what she doesn't know, if the
dead cannot know things

is that I am not Emily
—in any way

but, rather
much more
of a
Bukowski

and if the dead can feel
then
I think she
would feel sadness because

then, she finally would

know.

ravenous

I work in a toxic place
lead paint asbestos mold

dirty vents that haven't
been cleaned, since forever

toxic people
waiting to pounce on one another,
waiting for a misstep
a sullen mood or even

   nothing at all

glazed over
hung over &
tired

just waiting to devour whoever
dare
to just be stuck in the same
trap
in the same
  moment

I don't believe

calls were made, to loved
ones & friends
a small room existed just
for me, with soft pink
lampshades & morning light
beaming in warm rays
across my small nursery room
as diapers were stacked,
toys placed carefully, but
not stacked
in a soft white toybox

names were chosen,
plans were made, people
lined up to smell my
head

you didn't want me

life~

it's not Russian roulette if there
are no bullets,

it's not Russian roulette if there
is no gun

no, you see
there is no gun no bullets & no
sweat beading up
in the crease of my pants
causing me to slide around
just a little, as I wriggle
to get comfortable,
wiggle to arrange & rearrange
my ugly beige work pants

to soak up the puddle I sit
in
of sweat and dots of urine &
blood from my stomach that
leaks
   insisting it knows better
how I should eat, what & how
much I should drink
and what I think about when
the lids
—finally get heavy

it's not Russian roulette you
see, if as the lids
heavy now with drink &
drug and exhaustion
close and twitch

no
it's not Russian roulette at
all

under those lids that think
about the sweat and blood
& stink of Tuesdays
it's something worse   that as
the blackout comes, I nod
knowing this thing we live
the menial job and small talk
will not take me

it's not Russian roulette if I
never die
    completely

nothingness

I was drunk when they came
for me,
to keep me safe from myself,
he said
but that was a goddam
lie & everyone knew it

broken knuckles, bruised
beaten, wrapped tightly but
the silicone pink bracelet twisted
and rubbed under my cast

pushed, taunted & reminded
that I was no one
no one that could fight
no one that could win
and
no one that mattered much
to anyone

neighbors peaked out,
porch lights flicked on
I could see them
from my place,
face down on the hood of the
dirty police car
click click
went the handcuffs

it was summer not so long ago
really, but a lifetime for
her and many
but that didn't matter either

nothing did
or ever would again
not in any way that mattered
anymore

house of beauty

just three houses down
from my
pale green house
a magnificent dark red house
sat
regally
on a throne of both beauty &
possibility
on a street that never quite
fit in
with the rest of the city

it was a dead end,
in a time & place undefined by class
middle, less than that,
but
all otherwise, the same
more or less

except #44

it was the only house on the street
with a fence around the front

how rich they must be, I thought
to be able to have a fence
in the front

a small white sign with
black writing hung &
swung from a black post
behind that fence
with scrolled letters

Willie Mae's
House of Beauty

my mother would send me
if I was lucky, with 2 quarters
to buy us each a candy bar

that Willie Mae
would stock on a small shelf
in her makeshift waiting room
in her basement

I would look at myself in her big
mirror that sat in front of her 2
chairs,
that spun around

soaking in the smells of hair products, so different than my
own & listen to the women
talk about their lives
that somehow existed
outside
the House of Beauty

their hair so curly & beautiful
made my own
brown, flat hair feel lifeless
and
vanilla

she would explain to me why
she could not make mine, look
like theirs,
but still,
every time I walked down her
backstairs
quarters in hand
I dreamed that she could make
my hair kinky & shiny
while I talked & twirled

because
in the House of Beauty
anything was possible

or so I wanted to believe.

faces

they visit, not often but
   often enough that I notice them Now

usually when I am tired
or just waking up, when the light
is stretching out across my
small room in wisps and shadows
 I see their faces
normally hidden in their wooden veil

if I focus without blinking or shifting
or wondering why they are so visible now, I see them
like old friends they stay
—listening, if I chose to talk but
more often than not
we sit in silence these faces & I
as we have off and on since high school so many years ago
they
the faces in the paneling
remind me that there is always someone
 listening

Desi

I met him there, on a day that started too early,
one that drizzled & dripped & streaked the windows of the van
on the way to Tralee

I met him there, unplanned
somewhat unwelcome & entirely fateful

I was far from home, which was okay and something
I rather liked, but
no one was home when I returned,
happy to see me
which was okay, most days too, but
today I wished for someone to know me, someone to lend a
nonjudgmental ear & someone,
some one person to just want to get to
know me

I met him there, him reading the Irish Times, me
pretending to listen to music, both not wanting
to be bothered
—mostly

I met him there as the clickity clack train moaned on
towards Dublin and soft rain traveled down the window pane
showing me all the green
through the clear worm pattern the drips left,
before being washed away by others

ex patriot ex-husband ex business man ex cab driver

ex-wife ex grandma by default ex Republican ex drama queen

I met him there but I did not leave him
   there

I never saw him again
this man on the train
but as long as I live I will
always be on that train
with him on that rainy morning
enroute to Dublin

communion

I sat alone at the outside bar
one warm summer day
board shorts still damp
bare feet still coated in sand
that might never wash off
& couldn't help but notice
all the couples so happy

toasting each other, listening
to each other's tales
of the day

no one was listening to me
　　except, maybe
the faint day moon & the keeper of the tides
but I wasn't talking to either
of them
on this blue summer day

I sat there next to the
only open seat on the deck of a busy
beach bar

—most assumed I assumed
there was a friend joining me
so, it remained
　　empty

until
a newcomer appeared

he did not speak
I knew
he was there because I
heard

the bells, tied to his red high top
Chuck Taylor's
jingling as he casually
intently
sat down
in that empty chair

after a few oyster shooters &
shots of Patron
I asked the
wild white-haired stranger
about his bells

were they for purpose or decoration?
I inquired

neither
he smiled
as he ordered picklebacks
for both of us
and began telling me about
his morning surf
and I told
my tales to him
 & soon
my
loneliness disappeared
to the
salty ether
& I realized then just
why it was that he arrived
    with bells on

on being small~

what I will remember most
when I leave my small cluttered room full of old books,
surfboards & heavy memories
is not
the smell of stale wine spilled
on my tv tray, forgotten,
sticky & thick like gobs of
dried blood from forgotten
cuts
or the sounds of the city I
hear
—constantly   as I sit in an old
rocking chair by my small
window
and listen to fire engines &
street bikes racing carelessly without regard
and ambulances off to help &
other people's problems

no
what I will miss, should the
day come when missing is an
option
is the small sense of being
tucked in
under heavy crocheted blankets
with the souls of those
who shared this small comfort
in this small room
in a house that shrinks with
each exhale,

if that day comes and I live
in all the rooms of my own
house

what I will miss
is being
  small

morning wood

they come in—bright
full of hope & promise
the amber slants of light that reach
and stretch across my
dark paneled walls
towards what
   I don't know.

I imagine though
   blonde fingers on the other side
waking and stretching & reaching back for
their golden counterparts
and on those rare mornings
in those quiet moments
when the street is still
   silent
minus the busy bodied birds
chick-a-dee-dee-deeing
& dancing the leaves right off the giant American yellowwood
tree
  outside
my window
every single thing
is heard and seen and felt
spontaneously
serendipitously
until slowly the warm beams
retreat to the sun & the
place that exists
beyond the paneling
   and life is dark again

www.ingramcontent.com/pod-product-compliance
Lightning Source LLC
LaVergne TN
LVHW041559070426
835507LV00011B/1182